JUMP-STARTING A CAREER IN

HEALTH INFORMATION, COMMUNICATION & RECORD KEEPING

JEANNE NAGLE

ROSEN
PUBLISHING®

New York

Published in 2014 by The Rosen Publishing Group, Inc.
29 East 21st Street, New York, NY 10010

Copyright © 2014 by The Rosen Publishing Group, Inc.

First Edition

Library of Congress Cataloging-in-Publication Data

Nagle, Jeanne.
Jump-starting a career in health information, communication & record
keeping/Jeanne Nagle.—First edition.
     pages cm.—(Health care careers in 2 years)
Includes bibliographical references and index.
ISBN 978-1-4777-1692-2 (library binding)
1. Medical record personnel—Vocational guidance. 2. Medical records—
Management—Vocational guidance 3. Allied health personnel—Vocational
guidance. I. Title.
RA976.5.N35 2014
610.7306'9—dc23

                                                            2013011262

Manufactured in Malaysia

CPSIA Compliance Information: Batch #W14YA: For further information, contact Rosen Publishing, New York, New York,
at 1-800-237-9932.

CONTENTS

INTRODUCTION

Mention the phrase "careers in health care" and images of doctors, nurses, and lab technicians in freshly pressed lab coats and uniforms jump immediately to most people's minds. Yet there are a number of other career opportunities available in the health care field for people who aren't interested in pursuing a medical or nursing degree. In fact, many of these positions can be earned with no more than a high school diploma and some additional training. They are part of the growing career field of health information management (HIM).

For anyone wondering if a career in HIM is right for him or her, a quick overview of what a typical day on the job is like might be in order. There's no way to include every element involved, since each day can bring new challenges. Also, not all HIM jobs follow the exact same pattern. However, there are enough similarities that a rough scenario takes shape.

A few positions, such as medical transcriptionist, allow people to work from home or another remote location. Overwhelmingly though, health care positions such as these are conducted in a clinical setting—that is, a doctor's office, hospital, or clinic. The day starts early for most HIM professionals, since their job is to

4

Most health information management professionals are on the job early in the day to accommodate the schedules of doctors, nurses, and the patients being treated.

get everything in order before physicians and other clinical health care providers begin seeing patients. Setting up charts (records) for the day's patient visits, answering telephone messages, and checking on test results are some of the tasks that are completed early in the working day.

As the day goes on, HIM workers do their part to help as many patients as possible get seen, treated, and processed through the health care system. Medical secretaries and hospital receptionists greet patients and visitors, as well as get them started on paperwork that has to be filled out as part of the exam or treatment. Medical assistants take patients back to exam rooms and record their vital signs, all the while asking questions about their medical history and how they're feeling that day. Depending on the patient's medical condition or the procedure being performed, medical assistants may also perform certain clinical tests or give shots.

After a medical appointment is over and the patient has gone home, HIM professionals are still on the job, working to process patients' medical information. Coding and billing specialists process the forms and codes, which must be entered correctly, so that health care providers and facilities get paid. If medical coders and billers don't do their jobs quickly and effectively, the financial consequences can be very problematic, for facilities and patients alike.

Unless a scribe is assigned to follow a doctor around and take plentiful, careful notes, then most likely the physician's recorded notes will be sent to a transcriptionist. The transcriptionist turns voice recordings into written notes and sends them to the doctor's office. All billing and transcribed materials are most likely gathered in an electronic patient chart. The completeness, accuracy, and privacy of this chart are safeguarded by a medical records specialist.

The term "medical team" often refers to the various clinical professionals who examine and treat people who are ill. However, it could also easily be applied to the teamwork displayed by doctors, nurses, and the HIM professionals who offer support services. As this resource shows, every member of a medical team plays a role in assuring that the world is full of happy, healthy people.

Chapter 1

Health Information Management

A recent article in *U.S. News & World Report* proclaimed that health information management was a "field of the future." That statement might seem a bit odd at first. After all, physicians have been keeping charts and records on patients for a long time. Support personnel have been helping doctors keep track of all the information they gather. Yet technological advances and a push toward electronic medical files has put health information management squarely in the hot-careers spotlight. Professionals in this field are greatly in demand.

HIM Overview

Health information management is a very descriptive title. Professionals working in this career field manage all the health information concerning patients who receive medical care. Doing so means they assure that the information contained in each patient's medical record is correct and as up-to-date as possible. The data they collect and analyze includes dates and results of visits with primary care

The records that HIM professionals are responsible for are often quite large because they are full of detailed medical information.

physicians and specialists. It also includes medical history (including conditions and symptoms experienced), current medications, procedures and surgeries, test results, diagnoses, and recommended follow-up exams, procedures, and appointments. Some HIM jobs also involve billing patients for services rendered and receiving payments.

In addition to collecting and analyzing data, HIM professionals are also responsible for releasing patient information to other doctors on a patient's health care team, laboratories, and insurance companies. Obviously a person's medical data is sensitive information that should be kept private. HIM workers are charged with protecting the privacy of patients and their medical information.

Individuals who work in health information management are considered medical professionals. Most work in a clinical setting such as a doctor's office or hospital, and all are required to use and understand medical terminology. Most important is the fact that they take care of patients. Doctors and nurses offer direct, hands-on care; HIM personnel help make that happen by providing accurate information that health care providers need in a timely fashion.

Health Information Technician

HIM professionals are trained in a number of areas. Therefore they are capable of performing many different job tasks associated with patient information management. In large medical facilities, such as hospitals and private group practices with many doctors, HIM work is typically split among several people. Each of these professionals specializes in a certain task. In many physicians' offices, however, a single employee acts as a one-person HIM staff. A person who handles many aspects of HIM is often referred to by the general title of health information technician.

WHAT THEY DO

Primarily, health information technicians are responsible for collecting data pertaining to patients' health and

Taking careful notes and recording vital information about patient health form the bulk of a health information technician's day-to-day duties.

maintaining a complete, accurate medical record for each patient. Health information technicians gather together all the notes that doctors and nurses make while talking to and examining patients. They also report what doctors may write or dictate based on those notes. Also included in each patient's file are any test results that may come in, including imaging (X-rays, MRIs, CAT scans) and blood tests.

Once materials are gathered in one file, health information technicians are responsible for filing the information for safe keeping and easy access. For years this meant placing a paper-file folder in a file cabinet or mobile shelving storage unit. In the twenty-first century, however, an increasing number of health care providers, in the United States in particular, are turning to electronic health record (EHR) systems. EHRs contain the same information as paper charts, but the data is recorded and stored on a computer. According to a report published by Capterra, an online service that helps businesses select the software packages that work best for them, the most popular EHR software programs in the United States include eClinicalWorks, Care360, and Allscripts, to name a few.

EDUCATION AND TRAINING

High school students who are considering a career as a health information technician should concentrate on science classes, particularly biology and anything that covers basic human anatomy or the functions of the human body. Because of a surge in the number of health care facilities using electronic records, computer

ELECTRONIC HEALTH RECORDS

In 2009, the U.S. Congress passed the Health Information Technology for Economic and Clinical Health Act. This act offered monetary incentives for Medicare and Medicaid health care providers to switch from paper to electronic health records, referred to as personal health records (PHRs). Additionally, the U.S. Affordable Care Act of 2010 emphasizes the time and money savings to be had by adopting an electronic health information system.

Electronic health records are seen by many as a great boon to the health care industry. The time and money these largely automated systems save, and the ease with which the compiled information can be shared, are touted as reasons why electronic records are preferable to paper charts.

EHRs are not without their drawbacks, however. Getting a system up and running takes time, and there can be a steep learning curve for users, including patients themselves, who are unfamiliar with a system's software and database operations. Also of concern is the possibility that electronic systems' ease of use also makes it easier for billing fraud to occur.

classes would be a welcome addition to the course load as well. Outside of the classroom, future health information technicians might want to consider joining any medical or "future doctor" clubs their school has to offer.

Most people who apply for jobs as health information technicians have taken college-level courses in health information management and hold at least an associate's degree in that discipline. Employers are looking for people who have knowledge of the health care field and are "fluent" in medical terminology. A two-year HIM degree helps assure that a job candidate meets those requirements.

Graduating with at least an associate's degree is a prerequisite for certification as a registered health information technician. Only degree holders are allowed to sit for a certification exam given by the American

A student at Wheaton High School in Maryland performs a biology experiment. Hands-on learning in biology and related sciences is very helpful for those seeking a HIM career.

Health Information Management Association. Certification gives prospective job candidates an extra amount of legitimacy, since employers can see they are serious enough about the field to go the extra mile and boost their credentials. Also, certified health information techs may stand a better chance of being promoted and getting ahead in their careers.

WHAT THE FUTURE HOLDS

The *Occupational Outlook Handbook* and various regional colleges that offer health information management programs predict that the demand for HIM professionals could grow anywhere from 12 percent to 20 percent. Two factors are mentioned as possible reasons for this growth. First is the fact that people are living longer, and as they get older they typically need more medical services. The increase in people requiring health care services means a robust number of jobs in the health care field. Second is the move, particularly in the United States, toward electronic health records. Health care employers need to hire people who not only know how to perform health information technician duties, but are also able to fluidly operate the computer systems and software required to manage EHRs.

Information Therapy

A field that has been gaining ground since the interest in personal health records has peaked is information therapy. The abbreviation for information therapy is "Ix," which is meant to mimic the "Rx" abbreviation for medicine prescriptions. In other words, information therapy is considered a prescription for helping patients make informed decisions through the structured sharing of health and wellness information.

Patients have long relied on information conveyed by their health care provider regarding their particular well-being and any illness they might have. They have also used access to medical pamphlets distributed by health care workers, books, or articles in medical journals to investigate health and wellness concerns. Beginning late in the twentieth century, people turned heavily to Internet searches for health information. Each of these methods has its drawbacks, mainly the ability to remember verbal information or understand complicated medical jargon in written form.

Information therapy seeks to provide approved health information from a reliable, central source, namely a patient's health care provider or a member of his or her staff. Chief among the resources used to accomplish this goal is the personal health record, or PHR. (EHR is considered a more generic term for records that are available online. PHR refers to an electronic record that is individualized to a specific patient, complete with that patient's medical history and ongoing health and wellness concerns.) Toward that end, the American Health Information Management Association recommends that HIM professionals receive additional training that strengthens their ability to help patients access and understand their PHRs.

Chapter 2

Coding, Billing, and Claims

Among the duties performed by health information management workers is helping medical practitioners and facilities get paid for the services they render. Each time a patient is examined or receives treatment, a bill is generated to cover the cost of the doctor's time and expertise and any equipment or medicine used during these exams and procedures. Prices vary for these items. Additionally, a patient's health insurance may cover all, most, or only a portion of the expenses involved. Keeping track of medical costs, charging the correct amount for a variety of services, and figuring out who pays what on the overall bill are duties handled by HIM professionals known as coders and billers.

Medical coding and billing go hand-in-hand as the two primary steps in the health care payment process. In smaller medical practices, there may be one person who does both jobs together. Larger facilities, particularly hospitals, typically treat coding and billing as separate departments. These facilities usually have individuals who

Medical coders and billers work with patient records, medical insurance forms, and various machines that help them tally up costs and create accurate bills.

are dedicated coders or billers. In fact, each medical unit (pediatrics, orthopedics, emergency, etc.) of a hospital or similar facility may have a person or group of people assigned to cover its particular coding or billing duties.

Medical Coding Specialist

Looking over a hospital or doctor's bill provides clues as to what a coding specialist's job entails. Various boxes and columns of a typical request for payment contain numbers that may not mean much to the patient but reveal a world of information to accounting departments, insurance companies, and federal programs that help people with their medical costs. Those numbers are codes. They are carefully and thoughtfully put there by medical coding specialists.

WHAT THEY DO

The first step in sorting out payment for medical procedures is taken by medical coding specialists. In a way, coding specialists are translators. They turn complex diagnoses into simple codes that help ease and speed the payment process.

These professionals read documents that detail a patient's hospital or doctor visit, paying special attention to the tests that were performed and what diagnoses were given. Items that coders consult include patient charts. This is where doctors have written or input their notes on the visit. Coders also consult a superbill, which is a form that lists the procedures and diagnoses most likely to be encountered by staff at any given health care facility. (Superbills are more of a reference material or invoice than they are actually bills.) Codes are already assigned to each procedure and diagnosis on the superbill.

In smaller private practices, the treating physician often indicates what code should be used himself or herself. However, coders need to check superbill information against the doctor's notes to make sure the proper code is being used.

The notes that doctors and nurses write on a patient's chart are but one of the pieces of information contained in records maintained by medical records specialists.

After checking information and performing any follow-up necessary, medical coding specialists transfer codes from the superbill—noting any added or changed codes—to an insurance claims form. A claim is a formal written request that an insurance company pay a patient's medical bills. Beginning medical coding specialists usually rely on a booklet of codes agreed to by their medical facility and any insurers with whom the facility deals. People in this profession must also be careful about codes changing and new codes being added.

SUPERBILLS AND DRGS

A lot of information can be contained on one medical form. For instance, take the superbill, also called an encounter form, which is used by doctors in private practice and by hospitals, clinics, and other such health facilities.

Superbills contain basic identification data, such as the patient's name and personal information (address, age, Social Security number, etc.), the patient's insurance carrier, the name and licensing information of the medical professional who saw the patient, and the date of the medical visit. Then there are the coded descriptions of services that patients might receive. There are procedure codes and diagnosis codes on a superbill. Procedure codes, which are known as Current Procedural Terminology (CPT) codes, are provided by the American Medical Association. International Classification of Diseases (ICD) codes are generated by the World Health Organization. Both sets of codes are updated periodically.

Medicaid and Medicare codes are listed separately because these federally funded programs are billed differently. In fact, hospitals bill Medicare patients using a unique set of criteria known as diagnosis-related groups (DRG). Medicare insurance pays the same set amount for each patient within a particular DRG. The specialized billing process that determines which DRG a patient is assigned to starts with twenty-five main diagnostic categories that relate to individual organ systems (i.e. nervous system, digestive system, etc.) or causes of disease and illness requiring treatment (trauma, burns, pregnancy, etc.). From those twenty-five categories spring approximately five hundred specific DRG codes.

EDUCATION AND TRAINING

The minimum level of education required to become a medical coding specialist is a high school diploma. Taking as many business, science, and mathematics classes as possible is a terrific idea. These classes help build skills that medical coding specialists use every day on the job. Coders spend a great deal of time keying material into a computer. Technology classes that require hands-on experience with data input would add to career preparations.

Individuals who choose to receive more education in the field can find a college or university that offers a degree program in health information management. Classes that specifically cover medical coding are included in such programs. A person could get a bachelor's degree in health

Math classes—taken as a high school student or while in college—teach basic and advanced computational skills that are very helpful to medical coders and billers.

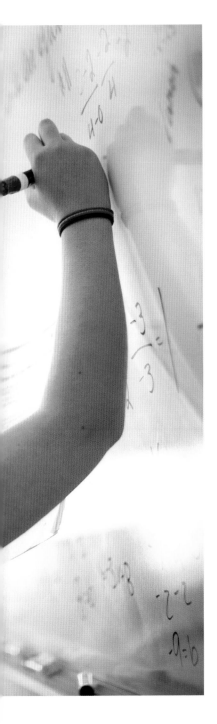

information management. However, a four-year degree is not necessary for this job. A two-year associate's degree provides plenty of information to give prospective coding specialists a great career start.

WHAT THE FUTURE HOLDS

The job outlook is very good for all health information management positions, including medical coding specialists. In private practices, which support from one up to a handful of doctors, the physicians themselves may do the majority of coding on superbills. Yet employment by large medical facilities should help coders remain busy for some time to come.

Medical Biller

Doctor's offices and hospitals are more than just places of healing. They are also businesses that need to make money in order to pay the people who staff them. The individuals responsible for making sure medical professionals receive payment for their services are known as medical billing specialists.

Medical billers may consult with doctors, medical coding specialists, insurance companies, and even patients to make sure the costs they are recording are accurate.

WHAT THEY DO

Medical billing specialists work with health care providers and medical coding specialists (provided the billing staff isn't responsible for coding as well) to gather and check information related to a patient's medical treatment. The sources they reference typically include patient records, doctor notes, and the superbill.

Once they have all the data in hand, they begin processing the paperwork or, more likely, inputting data into electronic forms associated with requesting payment.

MEDICAL CLAIMS ADJUSTER

Health insurance is designed to offset the cost of receiving medical treatment. As such, it is the job of insurance companies to pay a portion of medical bills on behalf of patients. The job of checking to make sure that insurance companies do not overpay or become the victims of fraud belongs to medical claims adjusters.

In a sense, medical claims adjusters are the flip side of medical billing specialists. Medical coding and billing specialists work on behalf of doctors, either in a private practice setting or for a hospital, clinic, or similar facility. On the other side of the coding and billing coin—working with billing documents on behalf of medical insurers—are medical claims adjusters.

While there are medical claims adjuster positions available for high school graduates, some companies either prefer or require at least an associate's degree.

The form that is submitted to insurance companies is called a claim. This claim is a request for payment by the insurer on behalf of the insured, the patient. People who do not have health insurance are billed directly. Patients may also be billed for any portion of the money owed not covered by their insurance. It is the responsibility of the billing specialist to investigate and resubmit claims that are rejected and bills that go unpaid.

When claims and bills are paid, medical billing specialists post, meaning record, the payments. As with issuing claims and bills, the recording of payments is done using billing computer software. Medical billing specialists also make themselves available to answer any questions and resolve any issues resulting from requests for payment.

EDUCATION AND TRAINING

According to the American Health Information Management Association, medical billing specialist is considered an entry-level HIM position. As such, the education requirements are not as stringent as they might be for a mid-level job in the field and definitely would be for a management position. What it boils down to is that a bachelor's or master's degree is not required to hold this job. However, most employers require that candidates obtain and maintain certification in an HIM discipline. Specifically, they require the registered heath information technician certification. In order to sit for that exam, applicants must hold at least an associate's degree in an HIM-related field.

WHAT THE FUTURE HOLDS

As with other health information management jobs, the medical billing field is expected to experience

A doctor uses a computer to chart the progress of a young patient. The growing use of electronic health records will have a ripple effect on how medical billers perform their jobs.

considerable growth in the coming years. Government regulations in the United States are changing the way health care facilities bill patients and their insurance providers, particularly with regard to the Medicaid and Medicare programs. Electronic health records are bound to affect the billing process as well. Therefore, it makes sense that well-trained medical billing specialists are going to be needed to keep up with all these changes for the foreseeable future.

Chapter 3

Administrative Support Staff

People who pursue a career in health care generally have a strong desire to help others. The wide variety of job titles within this field means that there are several different ways they can help. Clinicians, mainly physicians, are obviously hands-on practitioners. Many health information management personnel help patients by making sure their records and claims are accurate so that they are able to get treated and pay for clinician services. They don't deal directly with patients, but their work has a direct effect on people's health care.

After doctors and nurses, the health care professionals who spend the most time with patients are the administrative support staff. These are the workers who answer the phones, schedule appointments, greet patients, and make sure the office or hospital department operates as smoothly as possible.

Medical Secretary

Physicians are often judged by what is called their "bedside manner." This is an old-fashioned way of referring to

Support staff such as medical receptionists or secretaries have a great deal of interaction with the public, especially patients who require a trip to a doctor's office.

how doctors interact with their patients. These days, a patient's opinion of a doctor could be formed based on the "desk-side manner" of his or her medical support staff. The first people visitors encounter when they walk into a medical facility and the first ones patients speak with when they call a doctor's office, medical secretaries have the power to set the tone for each medical encounter. Those who work in a hospital setting may also be called patient registrars.

WHAT THEY DO

In many ways, medical secretaries serve as the nerve center of a medical facility. Information flows in and out from the front office where the medical receptionist is stationed. The information can be delivered over the phone, in the mail, or in person. Medical secretaries are often the first people to deal with patients and their information, no matter how it is conveyed. Scheduling appointments, answering the phones, preparing patient charts and records for examinations, accepting co-pays (costs not covered by insurance and paid by the patient), providing receipts and physician instructions, and helping

Acting in a pleasant, professional manner is a must for medical secretaries, whether they are handling phone calls, paperwork, or welcoming patients.

patients fill out forms are all examples of the medical secretary's job duties.

One of the unwritten duties of medical secretaries is to make patients and other visitors feel safe and welcome. This may seem like an easy enough task, but when a person is juggling other duties and dealing with several people at once—including some who may be very sick or worried—it can be hard to remain calm enough to smile and be pleasant while also being efficient.

People hoping to become medical secretaries should have excellent organization and time-management skills. A familiarity with common medical terms is a must, since communicating with patients about what ails them is a requirement. Finally, medical secretary hopefuls should have great interpersonal skills and a desire to help others.

EDUCATION AND TRAINING

Anyone who is a high school graduate meets the educational requirements necessary for a career as a medical secretary. Courses and activities that emphasize interpersonal skills, computer technology, math, and science should be a top priority when choosing electives and after-school clubs.

Being a medical secretary can be a gateway toward other jobs in the medical field, including office manager and health information technician. Those wishing to advance their career after starting off working in a doctor's front office are strongly encouraged to further their education. Employers prefer that applicants for management positions have a two-year or four-year college degree. Health information technicians need to have at

Taking science classes is a good idea for high school students wishing to become medical secretaries. Such courses in college are essential for anyone hoping to advance in the HIM field.

least an associate's degree to sit for the certification exam. People who have a degree in hand will be ready for promotion sooner than those who have only a high school diploma.

WHAT THE FUTURE HOLDS

High growth is anticipated for all receptionist and secretarial jobs, according to the *Occupational Outlook Handbook*. The sector that is responsible for most of that growth is in the medical field. Doctor's offices and hospitals will always have a need for competent, professional representatives working in their front offices. Those with previous secretarial experience, particularly that gained in a medical office, stand the best chance of finding long-term employment.

Medical Assistant

Doctors rely on support staff to help give patients the medical attention that they need and deserve. Sometimes a registered or licensed nurse is hired to prepare patients for tests and exams or perform certain clinical duties. More often, however, those jobs are performed by a medical assistant.

WHAT THEY DO

The job description for medical assistants is similar to that for medical secretaries, but with a little something extra. In addition to an administrative, or secretarial side, medical assistant jobs also include

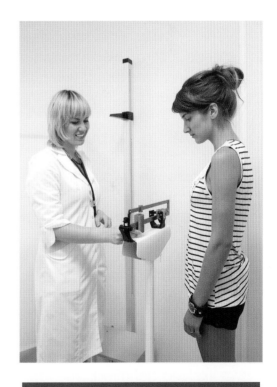

Medical assistants are responsible for certain clinical procedures during a patient's visit, including getting accurate weight and height information.

clinical duties. This means performing certain simple procedures and tests on patients.

Medical assistants help medical secretaries with reception duties and other office work. These individuals are typically the ones who call patients from the waiting room, check patients' height and weight, and take vital signs such as blood pressure and temperature before the doctor begins his or her exam. In addition to measuring vital signs, a medical assistant may perform other clinical duties. These include but are not limited to administering tests such as electrocardiograms, giving injections, conducting blood and urine tests, and preparing patients for outpatient surgery.

EDUCATION AND TRAINING

People who would like to become medical assistants can start preparing for this career while still in high school. Those who are interested should consider both sides of the job when choosing courses. Classes in business and office skills are good for the administrative side. Science and math prepare one for the clinical parts of the job.

A high school diploma or GED equivalency is technically all that is needed to become a medical assistant. Yet people who also have a medical assistant degree from a vocational school, college, or junior college are more likely to get hired. The reason is that degree programs in medical assisting focus on the skills needed for the job and offer practical, hands-on experience. This experience is especially important regarding the clinical aspects of the field. Employers would much rather hire someone who has taken blood pressure, drawn blood, removed sutures,

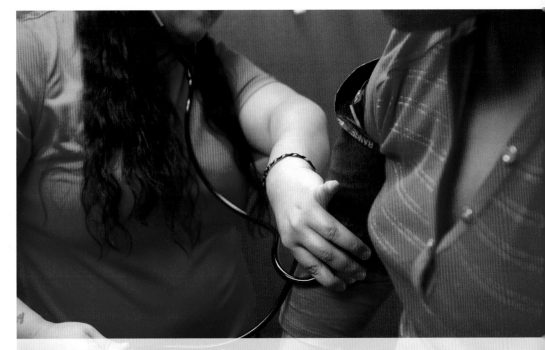

Being able to perform simple medical tests, such as taking a patient's blood pressure, is as important as in-class education when it comes to applying for a medical assistant's job.

and the like than take a chance on someone who would have to learn on the job.

Beyond learning-by-doing while working toward a degree, prospective medical assistants can look into getting an externship. Similar to a short internship, externships involve working (usually for free) in one's field of choice as a trainee. Medical assistant externships would place students in a doctor's office or hospital setting.

Certification is also an option that would be beneficial when seeking employment. Of the four organizations in

MEDICAL ASSISTANT VS. PHYSICIAN ASSISTANT (PA)

There is another medical professional with a job title similar to medical assistant, but that's where the similarities end. Like medical assistants, physician assistants perform clinical tasks in a hospital, clinic, or private practice setting. However, the level of medical procedures PAs can legally perform is quite a bit more extensive. Working under the direction of a licensed physician, PAs perform examinations, make diagnoses, and perform minor outpatient surgery. Also, depending on the laws where they live, PAs may be able to prescribe medication.

The level of education and training required is another difference between these two positions. High school is the minimum level of education a medical assistant must have in order to work. PAs are required to have at least a bachelor's degree. They must also complete an accredited PA training program. This usually results in their attaining a master's degree. PAs also must pass a separate licensing exam. To retain their licenses, PAs must take continuing education courses in their field and pass a recertification exam every six years.

Finally, PAs are not responsible for administrative office tasks, which are a large part of what medical assistants do. The salary level for PAs is quite a bit higher than that for medical assistants as well.

the United States that offer certification, only the American Association of Medical Assistants requires that individuals graduate from a vocational or college medical assisting degree program to sit for their certification exam. The other three allow high school graduates who are at least eighteen years of age take the exam.

WHAT THE FUTURE HOLDS

Individuals looking forward to long and steady employment as medical assistants are in luck. According to the *Occupational Outlook Handbook*, the medical assisting field is expected to grow much faster than average. Because of their ability to handle many different health care tasks across a wide spectrum, medical assistants should be in demand for some time to come.

Chapter 4

Records and Statistics

Documentation is an important element in a patient receiving proper health care. Without a proper paper trail—or, more likely in this day and age, an electronic trail—crucial information that can negatively affect a person's health can get lost. Tracking instances of certain diseases and conditions via medical records also allows health care providers to improve treatments and better allocate medical and technical resources used in those treatments.

The people who compile, input, store, retrieve, and share medical records and data play a vital role in keeping entire populations healthy. They are known in the medical field as records specialists and clinical registrars. While there are clinical registrars for several specialties, such as trauma and birth defects, by far the largest career group is cancer registrars.

Medical Records Specialist

Keeping track of a patient's symptoms over several visits can help doctors see a pattern of illness. This allows them

A medical records clerk works amid the stacks of alphabetized medical records in a California health center. Though electronic records are becoming the norm, many records clerks also maintain paper files.

to make more accurate diagnoses. Being able to reference a record of prescription medications a patient takes lets physicians and pharmacists avoid potentially harmful, or even deadly, drug interactions. Accurate, updated records are not only helpful for health care professionals; they can be lifesavers as well. The health information management workers in charge of these files specifically are called medical records specialists. Other names for this job include medical records clerk and medical records technician.

WHAT THEY DO

At first glance, the medical records specialist's job might seem pretty easy. Anyone who has worked with computers knows about putting material into electronic folders. Paper files are simply placed in file cabinets by alphabetic or numeric order. But consider the various types of information, coming from many different sources, that go into a patient's medical record: the patient's personal information and medical history, additional notes made by physicians and nurses, superbills, laboratory reports, prescriptions issued, and billing and payment requests and receipts. Multiply all that by however many medical professionals are treating any single patient and a mountain of information takes shape.

Medical records specialists are the keepers and guardians of each and every medical document pertaining to patient health care. Not only do they collect the information, they must also be able to locate and retrieve documents quickly and efficiently as the situation warrants.

Back in the days before computers, records clerks were also known as file clerks. The main part of the job consisted of filing folders full of paper in cabinets and other storage units. Modern medical records clerks, who are more commonly known as medical records specialists, still process a fair amount of paper, particularly in private-practice offices that haven't fully adopted computer record-keeping technology. The move in health care toward electronic health and patient records means that now records specialists are "filing" electronic folders onto computer hard drives and servers. All medical

Coding specialists reference books filled with hundreds of codes in order to make sure that what transpired during a patient's visit is crystal clear to clinicians and insurance companies.

records must be complete and up-to-date before being sent for coding.

Because the duties of one HIM worker may spill over into the job description of another, medical records clerks are well versed in a number of tasks performed by health care staff. Common crossover records specialist duties include tasks normally performed by medical secretaries, coders, and billers.

In virtually every developed nation, the way in which medical records are compiled, stored, and released is

HIPAA

The Health Information Portability and Accountability Act, commonly referred to by the acronym HIPAA, was made law in 1996 by the U.S. Congress. The first title, or section, of the act protects workers from losing their health insurance if they change or lose their jobs. The second title covers matters of security of electronic medical records and patient confidentiality.

The U.S. Office for Civil Rights (OCR) administers and enforces the second title's privacy and security rules, as well as the confidentiality provisions of the act's patient safety rule. Typically the OCR works with heath care facilities to fix any problems the latter has in meeting privacy and safety guidelines. In some instances, however, facilities that do not comply with the rules are subject to hefty fines. Each violation can incur a fine of $100 to $50,000 or more, depending on the situation and when the violation occurred. The fine limit for violations is $1.5 million.

dictated by strict laws and guidelines. Most of these laws are related to matters of privacy. Medical records specialists need to know inside and out every rule surrounding the information in their care. More than that, they have to re-educate themselves frequently to keep up with any changes to these laws and guidelines. Sharing such information with staff members at the health facility that employs them should also be in the medical records specialist's job description.

EDUCATION AND TRAINING

Subjects offered in high school that are related to what medical records specialists do on the job include biology, chemistry, communications, business, and computer technology. Securing an internship with, or otherwise volunteering to work in, a hospital or clinic's records department or doctor's office looks impressive on a résumé.

Some facilities might hire a person with a high school diploma or GED, combined with several years of experience in record keeping and/or in a medical office as a medical records specialist. Typically, however, an associate's degree from a university or college with an accredited health information management program is required to gain an entry-level position in this field. These programs focus on classes in communications, business, and, of course, record keeping. The last in this list most likely will include hands-on training in the latest health information management and medical records computer software programs.

Training courses for medical records specialists often include at least a smattering of basic coding and billing information. Learning about these health information management specialties ensures that prospective records specialists will be able to understand and even perform tasks on that end of medical records work as well.

Training on computer software used in medical offices is a major component of programs for health information management personnel, including record keepers.

WHAT THE FUTURE HOLDS

As part of the health information field, medical records specialist positions are expected to be available in record numbers for quite a while. Aging populations and a growing number of emerging health care facilities are just two reasons why individuals with this job title should continue to find work. The emergence of electronic health records also means that medical records specialists with current high-tech skills will be greatly in demand.

Cancer Registrar

There are many different types of cancer, affecting millions of people around the world. Keeping track of how prevalent or widespread given forms of the disease are, as well as of what research shows promise of eradicating them, can be difficult. Luckily, there are medical professionals who are dedicated to recording cancer data. This record keeping may help health care providers treat or even prevent cancer. These individuals are known as cancer registrars.

WHAT THEY DO

Cancer registrars are super sleuths of the health care field. Using various investigative tools of the trade, they search for clues as to how cancers behave in the human body, as well as how this disease in all its forms might best be treated or even eliminated.

Their job begins by locating patients with cancer. Registrars scour hospital, clinic, and private practice records to identify cancer patients within a defined area or region. Some cancer registrars limit their findings to patients who are being treated at a specific facility, most likely the same facility that employs the registrar.

After abstracting comes follow-up, wherein registrars compile and record information about the course that the cancer has taken in each patient. Information is gathered from all treating doctors and facilities, as well as the patients themselves.

Cancer registries are compiled by many different organizations and facilities. The National Cancer

Registrars Association (NCRA) estimates that nearly four thousand active cancer registries exist in the United States alone. Information from such registries is submitted annually to statewide cancer registries. Data in the state registries is used by state health departments, health care administrators, and others to determine the best ways to manage cancer. Strategies that depend on cancer registry data include the development of cancer screening processes, targeting populations for clinical trials, and advanced treatment for particular kinds of cancer.

In addition to their regular job duties, registrars may also monitor whether or not health care facilities meet standard guidelines for treating cancer patients. Many registrars also serve as consultants, who review how registries are maintained and the abstracts created by other registrars.

EDUCATION AND TRAINING

In the past, cancer registrars were usually people in other medical office staff positions who were trained on the job. These days, cancer registrars receive training in programs designed for them. A number of colleges and universities offer two-year degree programs with classes that focus on cancer data management, as well as medical terminology, statistics, and the nature of cancer as a disease. The majority of cancer registrars earn at least an associate's degree in this field or complete intensive vocational programs in registry management.

Certification is administered by the National Cancer Registrars Association. To be eligible to take the certification exam, candidates must have a combination of accredited training and registry work experience. In order to remain certified, cancer registrars take continuing education classes run by the NCRA.

WHAT THE FUTURE HOLDS

A 2005 Health Careers USA report indicates that the number of medical registrars entering the field tends to be lower than the demand for those positions. That's good news for anyone hoping to be employed as a cancer registrar. Another plus for career seekers is that the number of entities (government and health care agencies, insurance and pharmaceutical companies) that use registry information is on the rise, creating greater demand.

Chapter 5

Scribes and Transcriptionists

Health care providers are very busy people. The typical private-practice physician sees dozens of patients every day at the office. He or she also tends to patients who have been hospitalized. To make the best use of their time—so that they can treat the many people who need medical care in an efficient manner—doctors rely on individuals who are trained in medical documentation. These people record patient information by turning verbal elements of patient encounters into easily accessible written documents. Medical scribes accomplish this task by shadowing, or following, doctors during their hospital rounds or other patient encounters and taking notes for them. Turning verbally recorded notes and observations into patient chart information is the job of medical transcriptionists.

Medical Scribe

Ancient scribes were people (almost always men) who could read and write at a time when most of the populace

A medical scribe *(right)* follows a doctor on his rounds, a rolling computer terminal at the ready so that she can take notes on everything that happens as the doctor visits with patients.

could not. Their job was to record events of their time in writing, particularly regarding the all-important business of harvesting crops. Medical scribes of the current era are just as learned as their ancient forbearers, and their ranks include many women. They are able to read and write in a language unfamiliar to the masses: medical terminology. And just as early scribes were able to assist with the life-giving activity surrounding the harvest, medical scribes help doctors perform their life-saving work.

WHAT THEY DO

Medical scribes are more than just an extra set of hands in the exam room so that the physician can pay close attention to patients. They are indeed note takers. However, they have the advantage of having solid knowledge of medical terminology and basic biological processes. In fact, many scribes are either pre-med or medical students.

Medical scribes accompany doctors during patient encounters, listening to everything that is said and taking thorough notes according to the physician's request and need. Despite their training and education, these

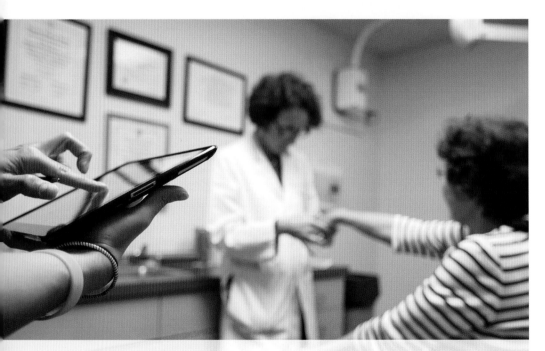

In order to take good notes, medical scribes must be able to understand complex medical technology. In some instances, portable electronic devices such as tablet computers make their jobs much easier.

professionals are not allowed to interject their own opinions or diagnoses into the electronic health record.

The position of medical scribe was created mainly in response to the shift toward electronic health records. Many physicians found it difficult to pay attention to and interact with patients while trying to type notes into a computer that operated within an unfamiliar software program. In keeping with their ties to the electronic age, medical scribes perform their work on laptops or other portable electronic information devices.

Many medical scribes work in a hospital setting and are especially valued in emergency rooms, where the pace is hectic. Large group practices are beginning to see the value of hiring these individuals as well. Working as a medical scribe is not a typical nine-to-five job. Since the majority of scribes work in a hospital setting, they are assigned to work the same hours, or shifts, that hospital personnel do. Typically, they are paid on an hourly basis.

EDUCATION AND TRAINING

The popularity of being a medical scribe as an up-and-coming career field has given rise to a number of training programs. At the core of most of these programs are classes in medical documentation procedures and medical terminology. Additionally, student scribes may be trained in basic health information management skills such as anatomy, diagnostic coding, billing practices, and privacy law.

Although there is no standardized training for medical scribes, most programs are built around a multistep process. First there is classroom (or online) learning, where

OBJECTIVE AND SUBJECTIVE MEDICAL INFORMATION

There are two types of information that medical scribes want to cover in their notes. The first is called subjective information. For each patient, they want to indicate the chief complaint, which is abbreviated as HPI (history of present illness). Also included is the ROS (review of systems), which lists any recent symptoms the patient is experiencing that may or may not be related to the chief complaint. Brief descriptions of the patient's personal medical history, family medical history, and any risk behaviors such as smoking that may affect the patient's health and well-being are also subjective information.

The second type of information is referred to as objective. Medical scribes also note what occurs during physical exams and record any test results, medicines, procedures run, medications ordered, or diagnoses made.

students take courses on how to function as professional scribes. Next, many programs require some sort of evaluation or supervisory process, where new scribes work under the close supervision of an experienced worker in the field. Finally, medical scribes are subject to reassessment by staff with the facility that trained them and are encouraged to take continuing education classes in health information management.

In the United States, the American College of Clinical Information Managers (ACCIM) offers scribe certification. Prerequisites include training through an accredited clinical information management program, completing one hundred hours of scribe service, and passing a written exam proctored by the ACCIM.

WHAT THE FUTURE HOLDS

Predicting the future of medical scribes as a career field can be a bit difficult. For one thing, medical scribes are a relatively new, and somewhat untested, addition to the ranks of medical information staff. Still, despite some initial resistance to having a scribe in the exam room, many physicians are seeing the value of having a scribe on their team. Overall, as part of the health information management career field, medical scribes should expect strong employment growth over several years.

Medical Transcriptionist

Medical transcriptionists are similar to medical scribes. They, too, are clinical documentation workers who prepare written patient information on behalf of doctors. Yet while the two jobs have similar goals, their methods and work environments are quite different.

WHAT THEY DO

As noted, transcriptionists create written reports regarding patient encounters. Instead of taking notes during an encounter, as scribes do, transcriptionists write out, or transcribe, information taken from a voice recording that a health care professional makes of his or her notes. Recording the notes for the transcriptionist is known as dictation.

Doctors and other health care professionals often dictate notes into a voice recorder after they have seen a patient. Dictated information includes exam summaries, diagnoses, test reports, procedures and medication ordered, etc. (Also included are identifiers such as medical record numbers that let the transcriptionist know in whose file the transcript should be placed.) Transcriptionists listen to these recordings and type what they hear. Written reports are then placed in each patient's personal health file.

Medical transcriptionists are trained to key information word-for-word that doctors dictate into digital recorders or other voice-transmission devices.

METHODS OF DICTATION

Technology has changed the face—or, more appropriately, the voice—of dictation. Several years ago, doctors would talk into a tape recorder, then send off the tape for transcription. These days, however, just as medical records have gone digital, so has dictation. Doctors now use digital voice recorders. Thanks to the Internet, they can now send audio files directly to a transcriptionist's computer, rather than send a physical tape.

Some hospitals and physicians groups use what is known as a clearinghouse for their transcriptions. Dialing a special number, they dictate their notes via phone, using prompts (pressing certain keys) to navigate through the system. Individuals hired by the clearinghouse phone in and retrieve dictated audio files for transcription.

Finally, some health care providers take advantage of voice recognition software, which turns their spoken notes into written pages of text on their computers. This takes typing out of the hands of transcriptionists, who instead merely proofread and edit the generated text.

EDUCATION AND TRAINING

The mechanical skills involved with medical transcription are relatively easy to learn. Being able to type quickly and accurately is essential. High school secretarial and business classes should help prospective transcriptionists increase their typing speed and accuracy. Today's transcriptionists must also be very comfortable with a wide range of technology, so computer classes are well worth taking, too.

Medical transcriptionists have to be well versed in not only English language skills, but also medical terminology. Taking as many English and communications classes as possible can help high school students strengthen their grammar and spelling. However, most schools don't consider "medical terms" a foreign language and therefore don't offer classes geared toward building a clinical vocabulary.

Medical transcriptionists have to write out verbal notes quickly and accurately. Computer classes train students to key in information rapidly and offer practice in the latest medical dictation and voice-recognition software programs.

Luckily, vocational schools offer medical terminology classes as part of their health information management training programs. Many such schools also offer training designed specifically for medical transcriptionists. In the United States and Canada, graduates of such programs are eligible to take the registered medical transcriptionist (RMT) certification exam, administered by the Association for Healthcare Documentation Integrity (formerly the American Association for Medical Transcriptionists). The organization also offers certified medical transcription (CMT) credentials to RMTs who have a minimum of two years' experience and pass the CMT exam.

WHAT THE FUTURE HOLDS

Unlike medical scribes, medical transcriptionists have been around a while in the medical field. Physicians are familiar with the benefits of hiring a transcriptionist or using a transcription clearinghouse service, so positions shouldn't be too hard to find. Transcriptionists with the ability to operate easily within electronic health record systems—a skill taught during training and refined on the job—and other dictation-related technology should prove to be the most valuable to employers going forward.

Chapter 6

Professional Development

Getting a job in health information management or clinical documentation takes planning, knowledge, determination, and drive. Believe it or not, keeping that job, or advancing in a career, takes all that and more. Just as a person needs to concentrate and work hard to find a job, and then work hard at that job, he or she also needs to put in some effort to be successful as an employee.

A Perpetual Interview

During job interviews, people tend to put their best foot forward. This means they are on time, enthusiastic, dressed appropriately, professional, and generally on their best behavior. Why would employers expect anything less of someone they have hired? After all, in addition to having excellent job skills, exhibiting all those traits helped convince them that the person being interviewed was right for the job.

Employees who not only keep their jobs but also get raises and receive promotions are overwhelmingly the

Good work habits are akin to performing well during a job interview. The same level of professionalism and positive attitude most people have during an interview is a plus in the workplace as well.

ones who incorporate many of the same attitudes and habits shown during an interview. Arriving at the office on time is an important first step. Showing up late too often without good reason is disrespectful of other people's time and sends a signal to an employer that the worker cannot be trusted to take the job seriously. Employees who work from home, which some medical transcriptionists do, are not off the hook for being punctual merely because they're not working in an office. Off-site employees should approach their day the same way as on-site workers by starting their work in timely fashion.

TIPS FOR GOOD WORKPLACE RELATIONSHIPS

One of the best ways to get along with coworkers is basically the same way a person would make friends—get to know them. Experts in interpersonal relationships recommend spending more time asking questions about another person than talking about oneself and actively listening to answers.

Respecting someone else's strengths does not mean a person has to hide what he or she has to offer though. Engaging in conversation, contributing at meetings, and suggesting solutions to problems earns people respect from their coworkers in return.

Wearing work-appropriate outfits is also important on the job. Clothes should not be too flashy or revealing, and they should fit well. In a medical office or hospital, certain staff members wear uniforms of some sort, including smocks, lab coats, and comfortable rubber-soled shoes (to reduce noise in hospital hallways and the chance of slipping and falling). While an employee may have no choice over the style of this clothing, he or she does have the choice to make sure everything worn is clean and in good condition.

The same attitude that a person has during an interview should be carried over into the workplace as well. Being polite and professional is not only expected by one's employer, but is also appreciated by patients, visitors, and coworkers.

Working Relationships

Not everything connected to an interview has to carry over onto the job, however. Obviously that nervous anticipation about getting the job should fade away soon enough. But so should feeling like the "new kid," at least once a new hire settles in and starts to develop good working relationships with others on staff.

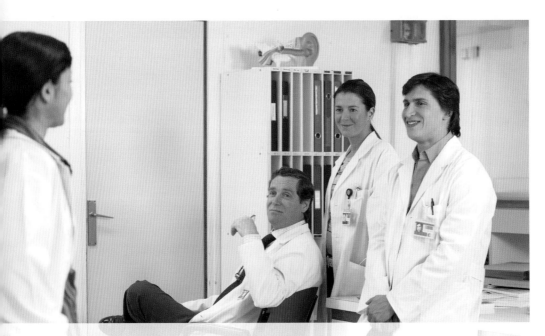

Working in a medical office affords employees the opportunity to interact with a wide range of people. Developing good relationships with coworkers can help make someone a valued employee.

Developing good working relationships is an important part of being employed, especially in a medical facility. Open communication and teamwork among coworkers are essential to protecting the health and well-being of patients. Beyond that, people who do not get along well with their coworkers could be thought of as uncooperative or "troublemakers," and may lose their jobs as a result.

The Benefits of Having a Mentor

Starting out in a new career field can be challenging, to say the least. Many people find that having a guide of sorts, someone they can talk to and bounce ideas off of, can be useful and wonderfully reassuring. That person is called a mentor.

Business mentors—as opposed to personal mentors, who are also called life coaches—offer career advice and encouragement. They help their mentees, or the people being advised, sharpen their existing work skills and seek out new skills to acquire. Typically mentors are people who are more experienced in an employee's particular field, but they could also be someone in a field that the mentee is working toward entering.

Finding a mentor doesn't have to be difficult, but it should be done thoughtfully. Experts recommend that prospective mentees think about what they hope to gain from such a relationship. The next step should be creating a short list of people who might make good mentors. Then it becomes time to choose. Explaining one's desire to have a mentor and why someone was chosen for that role should be part of any discussion with a mentor candidate. Individuals might want to consider "test driving" a mentor by asking his or her opinions and help on one issue and seeing how that goes.

This process can take time. People who choose to seek out a mentor need to be patient and not simply pick someone because it's convenient. It's also wise to reassess the choice of a mentor from time to time. People's needs and goals change, and it is possible that a mentor may no longer be a good fit.

Taking Advantage of Additional Learning Opportunities

Having a mentor is one way of learning while on the job. Certain parts of any job require learning as one goes. Every workplace has its own way of doing business. For example, health information management workers may be trained in one type of computer software, but the facility or office hiring them uses a different system. Learning by doing is an option in instances such as this.

Many companies, including health care organizations, offer opportunities to further employees' education and training in their career field. Employers make an investment in the people they hire. Helping employees further their education is not only a kindness to the employees, but also beneficial as a return on their investment. The more education and training employees have, the stronger they are as workers.

Formal learning opportunities could include attending local seminars or out-of-town conferences, or taking vocational courses. Some employers are willing to help pay for employees to earn an undergraduate or

Participating in continuing education programs helps health care workers stay current on medical advances. It also sends a positive message to their employers.

graduate degree in their field. Employees should consult their human resources department to find out what their employer offers by way of continuing education and training.

Getting Ahead and Staying Ahead

Preparing for a career takes hard work. It requires researching job titles within a field and finding a good match. Planning coursework around classes that will help a candidate land a good job in his or her chosen career is important as well. Gaining experience—through an internship, externship, part-time job, or volunteer work—is another key element of career prep.

Keeping a job requires work as well. Seeking out advice from a mentor and exploring new avenues for continued learning require patience and concentration. The same attention to detail that health information management workers bring to caring for patients is useful in caring for their careers as well. That means paying attention and attending to all the little everyday things that make someone a successful employee. These include showing up on time, appropriate grooming and appearance, and establishing respectful working relationships with coworkers.

It's not easy getting ahead and staying ahead in the workplace these days. Given the proper desire, preparation, hard work, and training, however, a successful career in health care information, communications, and record keeping is well within anyone's grasp.

GLOSSARY

claim To state that something is owed or due.

clinical Of or pertaining to analysis and diagnosis of a problem, as in an illness.

diagnosis A conclusion that is come to after keen observation and analysis.

dictation Speaking into a recording device for the purpose of later transcription.

medical chart The collected, recorded information on a patient.

mentor A trusted advisor, particularly regarding work matters.

patient encounter The interaction between a sick person and his or her physician.

prevalent Accepted or practiced over a widespread area or by many people.

registrar One who acts as an official record keeper for a company or cause.

scribe One who copies or writes information.

seniority How long a person has been in a field as well as employed at a particular employer.

superbill A list of the procedures and diagnoses most likely to be encountered by health care providers.

technician One who specializes in a particular subject, activity, or technique.

terminology Words and language used specifically in a particular field of study.

transcribe Turning the spoken word into written text.

trauma Pertaining to a very serious injury to a person's body or mind.

vocational Relating to the learning or honing of skills necessary for success in a career field.

American College of Clinical Information Managers (ACCIM)
60 Roseland Avenue
Caldwell, NJ 07006
(832) 224-6911
Web site: http://www.theaccim.org
The ACCIM offers educational programs, credentials and
    certification, and standardization of processes geared
    toward clinical information managers, otherwise
    known as medical scribes.

American Health Information Management Association
    (AHIMA)
233 North Michigan Avenue, Suite 2150
Chicago, IL 60601-5800
(312) 233-1100
Web site: http://www.ahima.org
Founded in 1928, the American Health Information
    Management Association is committed to providing
    members of this profession with opportunities for
    advancement through advocacy, education, and
    certification.

Association for Healthcare Documentation Integrity (AHDI)
4230 Kiernan Avenue, Suite 130
Modesto, CA 95356
(800) 982-2182
Web site: http://www.ahdionline.org
The Association for Healthcare Documentation Integrity
    offers hopeful and working medical transcriptionists a
    slew of services, including professional publications,
    continuing education opportunities, and certification
    assistance.

American Medical Billing Association
2465 E. Main
Davis, OK 73030
(580) 369-2700
Web site: http://www.ambanet.net/AMBA.htm
The American Medical Billing Association aims to provide
    industry and regulatory education and networking
    opportunities for its members. The organization offers
    free webinars, professional resources, an annual
    conference, and preparation for the Certified Medical
    Reimbursement Specialist exam.

Canadian Health Information Management Association
Suite 1404, 148 Fullarton Street
London, ON N6A 5P3
Canada
(877) 332-4462
Web site: http://www.echima.ca
Representing some five thousand certified and student
    health information management professionals across
    Canada, the CHIMA offers educational opportunities,
    events, and research within the field.

Canadian Institute for Health Information (CIHI)
495 Richmond Road, Suite 600
Ottawa, ON K2A 4H6
Canada
Web site: http://www.cihi.ca
The Canadian Institute for Health Information provides
    information concerning the nation's health system and
    the health of Canadians. The organization produces
    specialized and public reports and works closely

to raise awareness of health systems throughout Canada.

National Cancer Registrars Association (NCRA)
1340 Braddock Place, Suite 203
Alexandria, VA 22314
(703) 299-6640
Web site: http://www.ncra-usa.org
The National Cancer Registrars Association is a not-for-profit organization that focuses on cancer and tumor registrar education and certification.

Web Sites

Due to the changing nature of Internet links, Rosen Publishing has developed an online list of Web sites related to the subject of this book. This site is updated regularly. Please use this link to access the list:

http://www.rosenlinks.com/HCC/Comm

Abdelhak, Mervat, et. al. *Health Information: Management of a Strategic Resource*. Philadelphia, PA: Elsevier, 2011.

American Health Information Management Association Staff. *Pocket Glossary of Health Information Management and Technology*. Chicago, IL: American Health Information Management Association, 2009.

Bayes, Nenna, et. al. *Medical Office Procedures*. Columbus, OH: McGraw-Hill, 2011.

DeLaet, Roxann. *Introduction to Health Care and Careers*. Baltimore, MD: Lippincott Williams & Wilkins, 2011.

Ettinger, Alice G., and Pamela F Burch. *Medical Terminology for Health Careers*. St. Paul, MN: EMC Publishing, 2007.

Farhat, Kyle, and Nancie Cummins. *Claim Success! Absolutely Everything You Need to Know to Start a Successful Medical Billing Business and Create a Viable Career for Yourself*. Tucson, AZ: Wheatmark, 2008.

Gartee, Richard. *Health Information Technology and Management*. Upper Saddle River, NJ: Pearson, 2010.

Gilmore, Diane. *Medical Transcription Fundamentals: Where Success Takes Root*. Baltimore, MD: Lippincott Williams & Wilkins, 2012.

Green, Michelle A., and Mary Jo Bowie. *Essentials of Health Information Management: Principles and Practices*. Independence, KY: Cengage Learning, 2010.

Houser, Helen, and Terri Wyman. *Administrative Medical Assisting: A Workforce Readiness Approach*. Columbus, OH: McGraw-Hill, 2011.

Jones, Molly. *Top 10 Tips for Planning for a Career*. New York, NY: Rosen Publishing Group, 2012.

Judson, Karen, and Carlene Harrison. *Law & Ethics for Medical Careers.* New York, NY: McGraw-Hill, 2007.

Jurek, Jean, et.al. *McGraw-Hill Medical Coding: An Introduction.* New York, NY: McGraw-Hill, 2008.

Krager, Carole, and Dan Krger. *HIPAA for Health Care Professionals.* Independence, KY: Cenage Learning, 2008.

Martin, Diann L. *Kaplan Medical Assistant Exam Review.* New York, NY: Kaplan Publishing, 2010.

Martinez, Anne. *Medical Transcription for Dummies.* Hoboken, NJ: John Wiley and Sons, Inc., 2012.

Odom-Wesley, Barbara. *Documentation for Medical Records.* Chicago, IL: American Health Information Management Association, 2008.

Shiland, Betsy J. *Mastering Healthcare Terminology.* St. Louis, MO: Elsevier Mosby, 2012.

Wischnitzer, Dr. Saul, and Edith Wischnitzer. *Top 100 Health Care Careers.* Indianapolis, IN: JIST Publishing, 2011.

BIBLIOGRAPHY

American Health Information Management Association. "Health Information Careers: Frequently Asked Questions." AHIMA. Retrieved March 6, 2013 (http://www.hicareers.com/Health_Information _101/faqs.aspx).

American Medical Association. *Health Care Careers Directory 2012–2013*. Chicago, IL: American Medical Association, 2012; pp. 197–198, 203–204.

Bureau of Labor Statistics. *Occupational Outlook Handbook* online. Retrieved March 6, 2013 (http://www.bls.gov).

Burns, Karen. "13 Tips on Finding a Mentor." *U.S. News & World Report*. Retrieved March 6, 2013 (http://money.usnews.com/money/blogs/outside-voices -careers/2010/01/13/13-tips-on-finding-a-mentor).

Burrington-Brown, Jill. "Information Therapy: A New Interest for HIM." *Journal of AHIMA* 80, No. 6, June 2009; pp. 28–31.

Capterra, Inc. "The 20 Most Popular EMR Software Solutions." Retrieved March 6, 2013 (http://www .capterra.com/infographic-top-20-emr-software -solutions).

Dolan, Marsha, et. al. "Consumer Health Informatics: Is There a Role for HIM Professionals?" *Perspectives in Health Information Management*, Vol. 6. Retrieved March 6, 2013 (http://perspectives.ahima.org /consumer-health-informatics-is-there-a-role-for-him -professionals).

Ferguson. *Exploring Health Care Careers*. New York, NY: Infobase Publishing, 2006.

Hareyan, Armen. "Healthcare Boom Increases Demand for Medical Support Staff." EmaxHealth.com. Retrieved March 6, 2013 (http://www.emaxhealth .com/1/38/27674/healthcare-boom-increases -demand-medical-support-staff.html).

HealthIT.gov. "Learn EHR Basics." Retrieved March 6, 2013 (http://www.healthit.gov/providers -professionals/learn-ehr-basics).

Mariani, Matthew. "You're a What? Cancer Registrar." *Occupational Outlook Quarterly*, Fall 2003, Vol. 47, Number 3. Retrieved March 6, 2013 (http://www.bls.gov/opub/ooq/2003/fall /yawhat.htm).

McCutcheon, Maureen, and Mary Phillips. *Exploring Health Careers*. Clifton Park, NY; Thompson Delmar Learning, 2006.

MedicalAssistantSalaryData.org. "Become a Medical Assistant." Retrieved March 6, 2013 (http://www .medicalassistantsalarydata.org).

New York State Department of Health. "Chronic Disease Research Tools—Disease Registries." Retrieved March 6, 2013 (http://www.health.ny.gov/diseases /chronic/diseaser.htm).

Porterfield, Deborah. *Top Careers in Two Years: Health Care, Medicine, and Science*. New York, NY: Ferguson Publishing, 2008.

Scribe America. "Prospective Scribes FAQ." Retrieved March 6, 2013 (https://www.scribeamerica.com /FAQ.html).

SearchHealthIT.com. "Registered Health Information Technician (RHIT)." Retrieved March 6, 2013 (http://

searchhealthit.techtarget.com/definition/registered
-health-information-technician-RHIT).
U.S. Office of Personnel Management. "Medical Records
Technicians Series." Retrieved March 6, 2013
(http://archive.opm.gov/fedclass/gs0675.pdf).
Wilson, Robert F. *Success Without College: Careers in
Healthcare*. Hauppauge, NY: Barron's Educational
Series, 1999.
Wisconsin Area Health Education Centers. "Healthcare
Occupations: Medical Coding Specialist." Retrieved
March 6, 2013 (http://wihealthcareers.org/Career_
occ_view.cfm?o_id=33).

INDEX

About the Author

Jeanne Nagle is a writer and editor based in upstate New York. Among her works for Rosen are several career-oriented books, including *Careers in Television*, *Choosing a Career as a Coach*, and *Careers in Internet Advertising and Marketing*.

Photo Credits

Cover (figure) © iStockphoto.com/jsmith; cover and interior pages (files) Jupiterimages/Photos.com/Thinkstock; cover, back cover, p. 1 (background pattern) HunThomas/Shutterstock.com; pp. 4–5 (background) sfam_photo/Shutterstock.com; p. 5 (inset) Wavebreak Media/Thinkstock; p. 9 Medioimages/Photodisc/Digital Vision/Thinkstock; p. 11 Creatas/Thinkstock; pp. 14–15 The Washington Post/Getty Images; pp. 19, 35 iStockphoto/Thinkstock; p. 21 Joe Rimkus Jr./MCT/Landov; pp. 24–25, 52 Boston Globe/Getty Images; p. 26 Jochen Sand/Digital Vision/Thinkstock; p. 29 Chris Seward/MCT/Landov; pp. 31, 56 Comstock/Thinkstock; p. 32 Hemera/Thinkstock; p. 34 Purestock/Thinkstock; p. 37 John Moore/Getty Images; p. 41 Phil McCarten/Reuters/Landov; p. 43 Ingram Publishing/Thinkstock; p. 46 Jetta Productions/Lifesize/Thinkstock; p. 51 Benjamin Brink/The Oregonian/Landov; p. 58–59 PhotoAlto/Alix Minde/Getty Images; p. 62 Photo-Biotic/Photolibrary/Getty Images; p. 64 Michael Blann/Digital Vision/Thinkstock p. 67 © AP Images.

Designer: Michael Moy; Editor: Nicholas Croce; Photo Researcher: Amy Feinberg